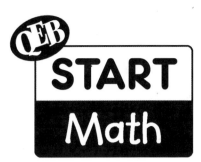

START
Math

Numbers
Book 2

Ann Montague-Smith

QEB Publishing

Copyright © QEB Publishing, Inc. 2004

Published in the United States by

QEB Publishing, Inc.
23062 La Cadena Drive
Laguna Hills
Irvine
CA 92653

Library of Congress Control Number: 2004102071

ISBN 1-59566-029-1

Written by Ann Montague-Smith
Designed and edited by The Complete Works
Illustrated by Jenny Tulip
Photography by Steve Lumb and Michael Wicks

Creative Director Louise Morley
Editorial Manager Jean Coppendale

Printed and bound in China

With thanks to:

Contents

1 more and 1 fewer 4

Adding 2 sets 6

Adding 3 sets 8

Counting up 10

Hiding a quantity 12

Making totals 14

Count what is left 16

Shopping 18

I know about totals to 10 20

Supporting notes for adults 22

Suggestions for using this book 24

1 more and 1 fewer

5 people are on the bus. 1 more gets on.
How many are on the bus now?

At the next bus stop, 8 people are now on
the bus. 1 gets off. How many are left on the bus?

4

4 + 1 + 1 = 6

Challenge

Ask a friend to count a small handful of blocks. Say, "What if there were 1 more or 1 fewer? How many then?"

Adding 2 sets

How many donuts can you see?

How many cupcakes are there?

How many donuts and cupcakes are there in all?

How many muffins and cookies are there in all?

Challenge

Use some play dough.
Make some donuts
and cupcakes.
How many donuts
are there?
How many cupcakes?
How many treats
did you make
in all?

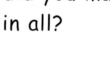

Adding 3 sets

How many hats, scarves and coats can you see in each set?
How many hats, scarves and coats in all?

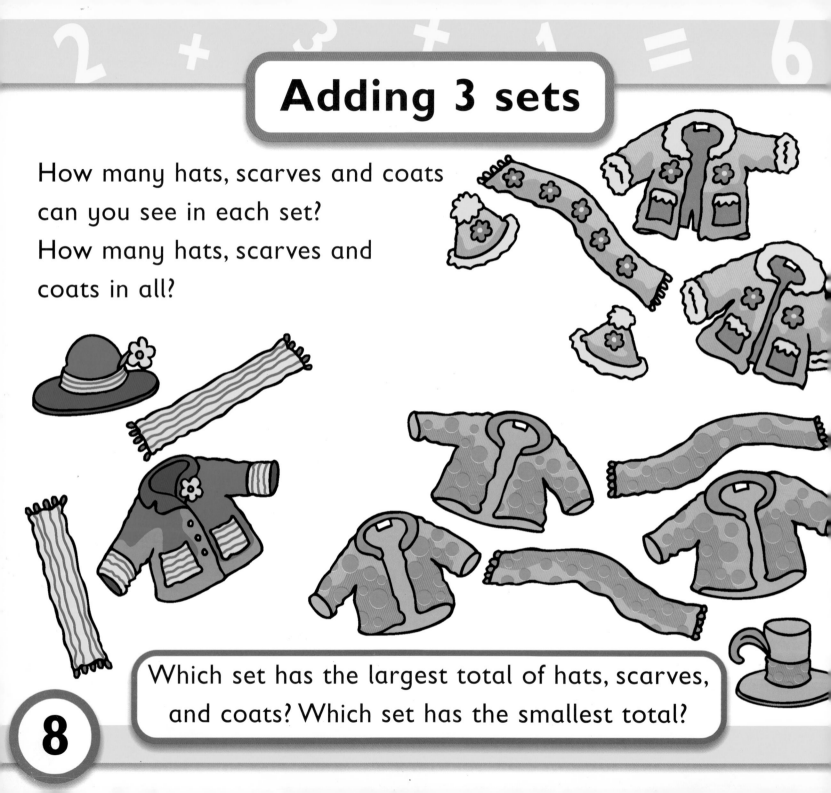

Which set has the largest total of hats, scarves, and coats? Which set has the smallest total?

Challenge

Draw 3 different sets of clothes. How many clothes are there in each set? How many clothes did you draw in all?

Counting up

Play this game with friends. You will each need a token for the track. You will also need a token for the chooser. Throw a token onto the chooser. Move that number on the track. The first one to reach 10 is the winner.

start

1 2 3 4 5

If you land on 4, how many do you need to move to 6?

10

4 + 1 + 1 = 6

6 7 8 9 10 finish

What number did you start on?
What number are you on now?
So how many did you count up?

11

Hiding a quantity

The magician has 3 rabbits in the hat.

Now he puts 1 more rabbit into the hat.

How many rabbits are in the hat in all?

The magician has 4 rabbits in the hat. He puts 2 more in. How many are there in all now?

$$4 + 1 + 1 = 6$$

Challenge

Put some tokens into a bag and say how many. Take some more and ask a friend to count them. Put these into the bag too. Now ask, "How many tokens are there in the bag?"

Making totals

Find 2 sets of space bugs that total 6.

How many different ways can you find to total 6?

Can you find 2 sets that total 5?

Count what is left

See if you can figure out what is left.

Maria eats 4 sundaes.
How many are left?

Tom eats 1 cupcake.
How many are left?

4 + 1 + 1 = 6

Challenge

Take 6 tokens and hide some under a cup. Show how many are left. Ask a friend, "How many tokens are hidden?"

Sam eats 2 cookies. How many are left?

Anna eats 2 lollipops. How many are left?

Shopping

Get 10 play money coins.
Choose a toy. Put the correct
number of coins on that toy.
How much did you spend?
How many coins do you have left?

2

4

10

6

5

Take the coins off. Now buy another toy.
How many coins do you have left now?

4 + 1 + 1 = 6

7

9

1

8

3

Challenge
Choose 2 toys to buy.
How much did they cost?
How many coins do
you have left?
Can you find different
ways to do this?

19

I know about totals to 10

Put 1 token onto each treasure chest. You and a friend will each need a token. Take turns to roll a die. Move that number of spaces. If you land on a treasure chest, take the token. The winner is the one who takes the most tokens.

How many tokens do you have? How many does your friend have? How many tokens are there in all?

Challenge

Play the game again with 10 tokens each.

Every time you land on a treasure chest, put a token onto the chest. Say how many tokens you have now. The winner is the first person with no tokens left.

21

Supporting notes for adults

1 more and 1 fewer – pages 4-5

If the children cannot yet add on 1, suggest to them that they use the line of flowerpots to count 1 more, or back 1. Suggest other numbers of people on the bus, with 1 more or 1 fewer, such as 6 people, 4 people… up to 9 people.

Adding 2 sets – pages 6-7

Ask the children to combine different sets of treats. They can count one set, then count the second set. Finally, they can count all of those treats to find the total.

Adding 3 sets – pages 8-9

The children may find it easier at this stage to count each set, then to count them all. Encourage them over time, to count on mentally from the total of the first set of hats.

Counting on – pages 10-11

Have the children say what number they must move their token to by asking them to count up in their heads. If they find this difficult, let them count up by moving their token along the track, then together count up mentally: start on 4, die shows 2, so 4, 5, 6.

4 + 1 + 1 = 6

Hiding a quantity – pages 12-13

Encourage the children to count up from the number that is hidden in the hat.
If they find this difficult, count together. Suggest other numbers of rabbits in the hat,
and to be added to it. Keep the totals to a maximum of 6 to begin with.

Making totals – pages 14-15

If children find this activity hard, give them 8 board game tokens and ask them
to make 2 sets in different ways. Then try the activity on the page again.

Count what is left – pages 16-17

Encourage the children to count all of the pieces of food in the picture, then to count
the ones that have been eaten. If they cannot say how many are left, suggest that they
cover those that have been eaten with a token, and count those they can still see.

Shopping – pages 18-19

Encourage the children to count out the coins for each toy and say how
much that is. Then they can count how many coins are left. Encourage them to put this
into a number sentence: "I have 10 coins; my drum cost 3 coins; now I have 7 coins left."

I know about totals to 10 – pages 20-21

Ask questions such as, "How many coins do you have? How many does … have? So how many coins
do you have in all? How many more are there still on the board?"

Suggestions for using this book

Children will enjoy looking through the book and talking about the colorful pictures. Sit somewhere comfortable together. Read the instructions to the children, then encourage them to take part in the activity and check whether or not they understand what to do.

In this book, children are encouraged to work practically to solve addition and subtraction problems. They are introduced to the strategy of counting up from a quantity in order to find a total. For example, when adding 3 and 5, they could begin by counting the five: 1, 2, 3, 4, 5. Now they count up from 5 for three more: 6, 7, 8. So 8 is the total. At first, children will count up from either quantity. You might suggest that they try counting up from the smaller quantity. Then try it the other way around. Of course, they will find the result is the same. Now suggest that they try counting up from the larger quantity. This is the easier way to do it!

Shopping using coins is introduced. Use play money coins worth 1 unit each to begin with. Children can then use counting to show what they spend and how much money is left.

DISCARD